Flowers of Unknown Origin
Dance of the Forbidden Vegetables

by

Lydia Cooley Freeman

Lydia, 1971

Photo by Deason

Flowers of unknown origin

Dance of the Forbidden vegetables

Lydia Cooley Freeman

Contents

To Lydia's spirit

and all her inner and outer friends

Foreword

Over the last 25 years of her life, Lydia worked on a set of poems she called her "haikus." She knew, of course, that they were not in the precise form of the traditional Japanese 5-7-5 pattern of phonetic units, and this kept her rewriting and reworking them over and over again.

From 1996 to the spring of 1998 (at age 91), Lydia worked less on her haikus, but every night she would draw a "doodle" — as she called it — expressing her feelings and moods at the end of the day. She often discussed the idea of putting some of her haikus together with an appropriate doodle. When it became apparent that she could no longer work on her haikus and doodles, a group of her friends and I put together a small book of her poetry and sketches in a limited printing. Fortunately, we completed this book in time to show Lydia a few months before she died. Her smile told us she was deeply delighted. Lydia passed away in Switzerland on August 5, 1998.

In those last years, Lydia also worked on several larger watercolors with a few selected haikus and music composed by a friend, David Eldred. With these too, she was never satisfied and kept beginning anew. For this new edition of the originalyl privately printed book, I have included a selection of these larger watercolors with their poems in her own script, just as she left them, unfinished. In one note she called these creations, "The sorrows of my heart that I have never told." I am sharing these as a record of one woman's confrontation and dance with her inner soul for all who would like to partake of her "forbidden" vegetables.

Roy Freeman
Lucerne, Switzerland
April 2022

For more on Lydia, her paintings and illustrations, visit
www.lydiafreeman.com

Being eighty

The subject is being eighty
the blue hour
alone on this ebony pebbled beach

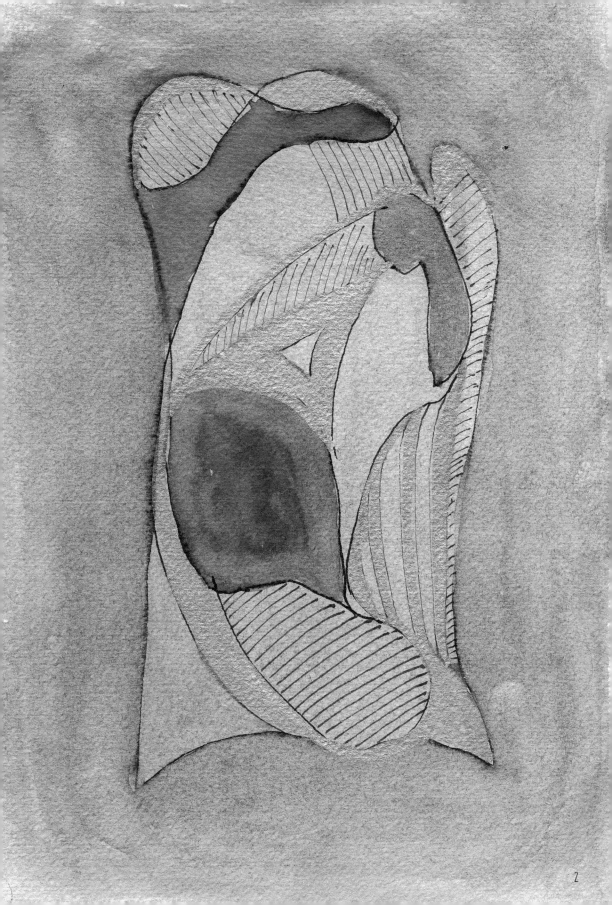

2

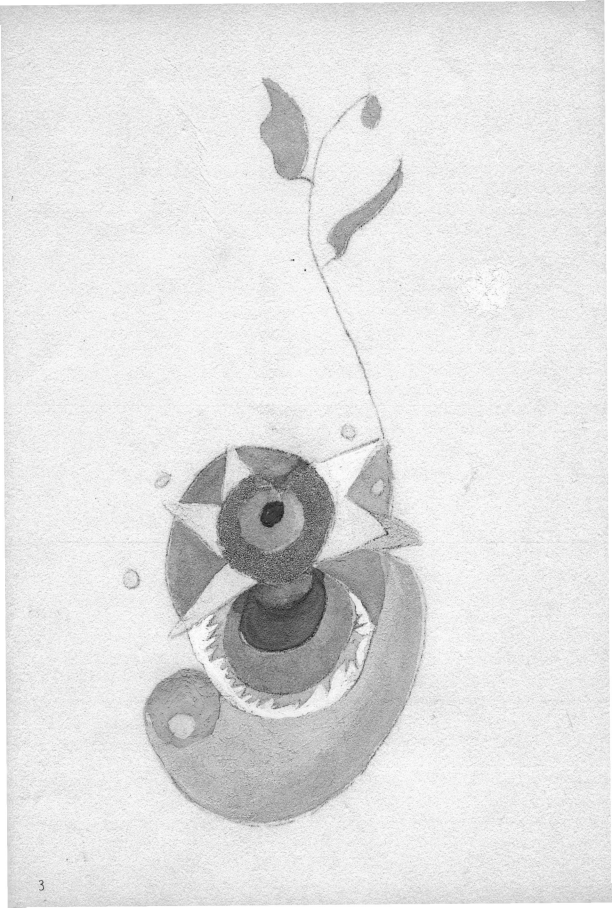

3

The garden fence

Garden fence awry
mischievous winds
torment the dying leaves
and the flowers of unknown origin
are crying again

Was it fate

Was it fate or caring
that prompted him to wait
or was it a dance in the flowering meadows
along the way

You thought I loved you

You thought I loved you
so did I
but knowing you revealed I knew not myself
rather than break your heart
I dared to leave
and broke my own instead

The one with the graying hair

The one with the graying hair
who naively thought
she was to become more human
the world of human was to become more humane

Thursday

6

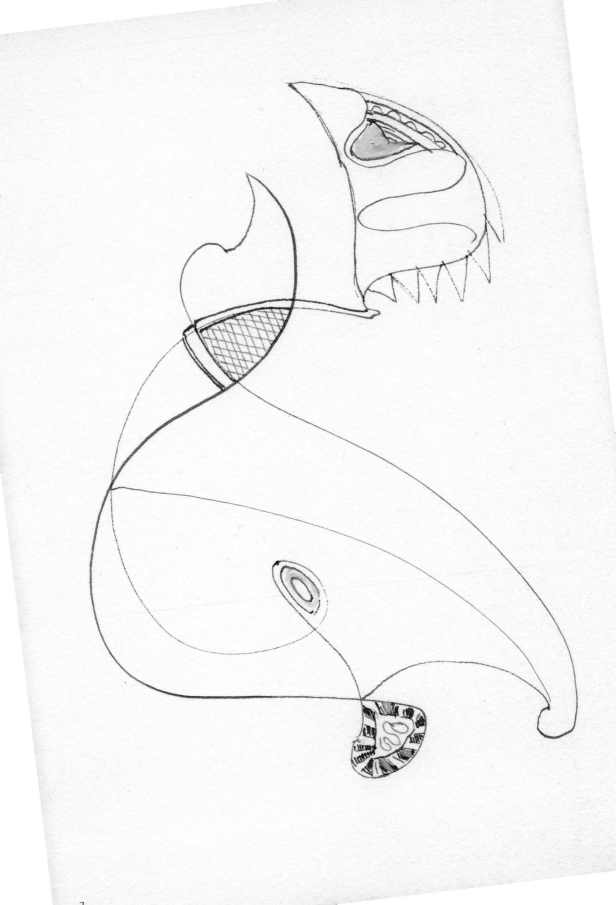

This solitude

I asked for it
this solitude
unaware that my other selves would come along
some I had not met before
and will not have the time to know

How many petals

How many petals
does a rose have
the number of my many selves
not friendly with each other
making wretched company for
their guardian host

Bamboo

Errant but with grace
bamboo belying its strength
invades my garden

No wine

No wine to soothe the beasts
of day

no wine to tame the dragons
of twilight

no midnight snack
to snare the ghosts
of dawn

no wonder I dream
of pomegranates

no wine
to sooth the beasts
of day
no wine to tame the dragons
of twilight

no midnight snack
to snare the ghosts
of dawn

no wonder I dream
of pomgranates

No net

There is no bridge
to the far side of love
taut with risk
only a lone tightrope
spans the abyss
once committed
I brave crossing it
dear God
there is no net

While angels prevail

Shall I go out
while angels prevail
or endure until
dark despair enslaves
no matter —
the answers are within

This carousel

I should be prepared
to get off this carousel
with as much grace
as possible

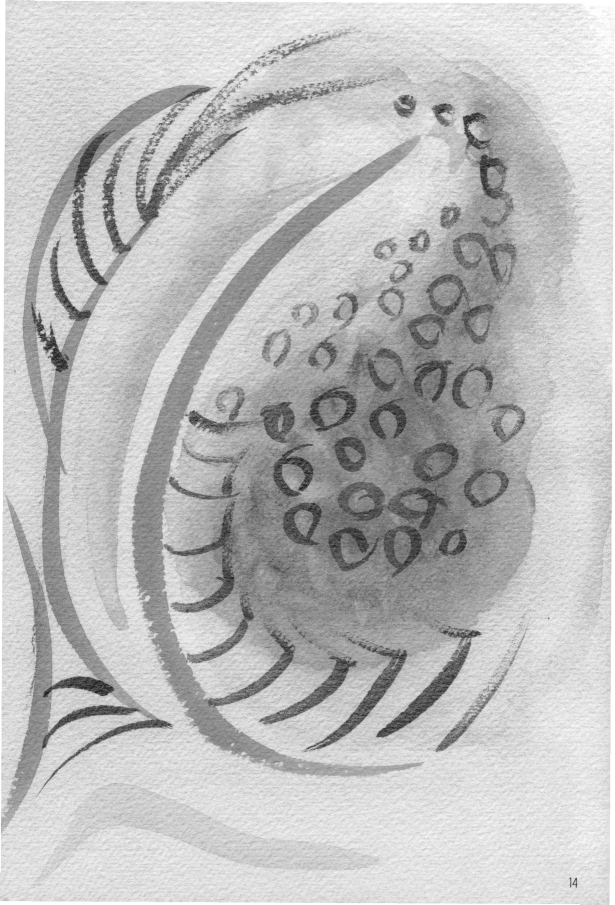

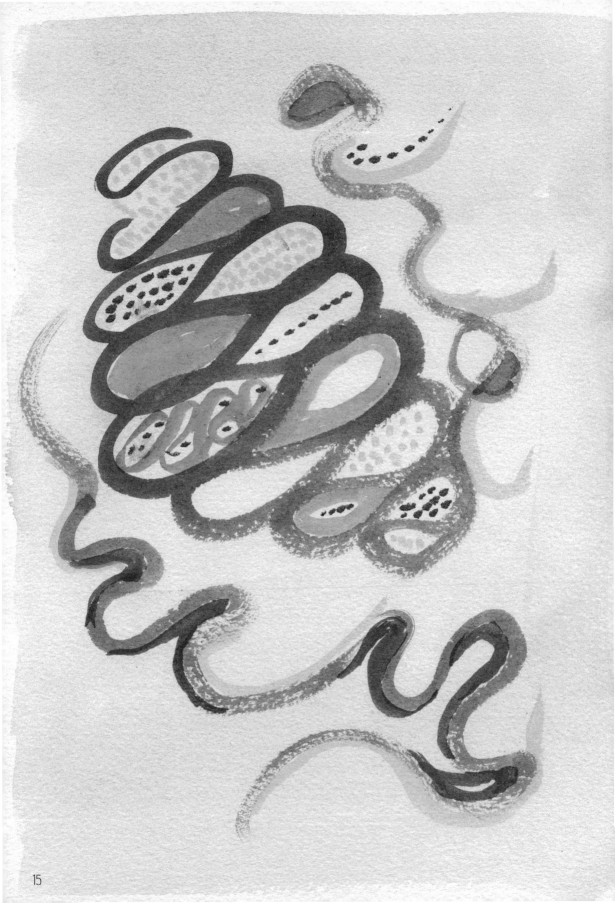

Square stones

square stones do not skim
neither do they sink
round ones skip on the surface
but they sink
you mean it was you
wanting to come in

Picnic basket

Picnic basket packed
delectable delights
by the seashore
perhaps the sands are warm
oh, but I forgot
two are needed

Punctual

Punctual
on the unimportant
tardy
on the essentials

Where does the heart dwell

Where does the heart dwell
once it departs
the inner realm
and echoes remindings back
to wound with
haunting song

Where
does the heart dwell
o once it departs
the inner realm
and echos remindings back
to wound with
haunting song

Tell him today

Tell him today
your love
he may not be here tomorrow
and eternity is not far away

There was a time

There was a time
when the azure skies were innocent
now, only compliant trusting morning glories
turn their petalled loneliness
heavenward
along my garden path
a warring activity

I've heard it said

I've heard it said
that at the moment of death
one's life passes in review before exodus
be that the case, I have died a thousand deaths
the loneliness of being the one
on the other hand

Friendship

Secret death of a friendship
slowly tarnished by silent misunderstandings
festering in shadowed crevices
and fatally flawed from the beginning
by needs expecting fulfillment

Was it preordained

Was it preordained
that there would always be misery
or is it that good exists
only when evil its opposite
is present

Wrap me in the fabric

Wrap me in the fabric of my past
when the future beckons like the sunrise
where I met you
in the garden of the blue hyacinth

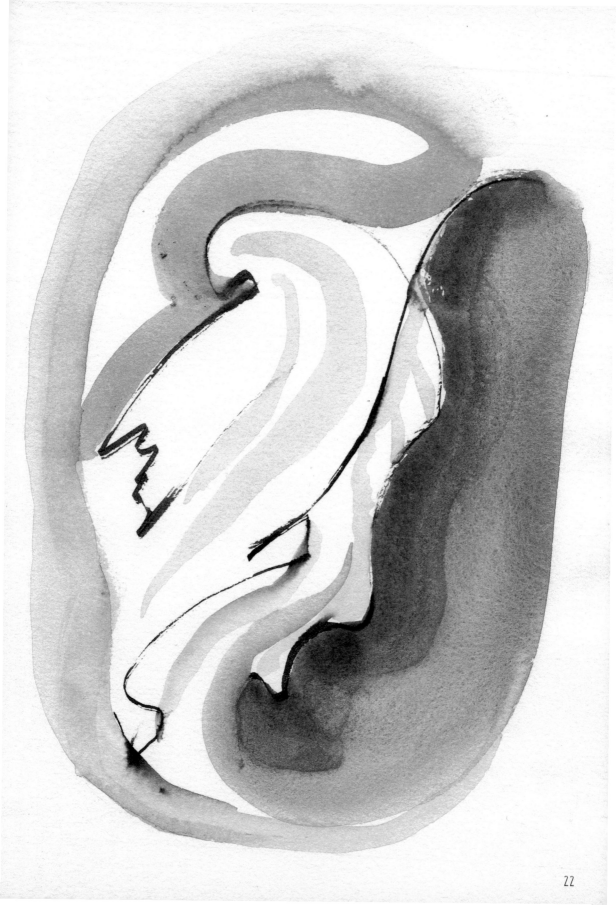

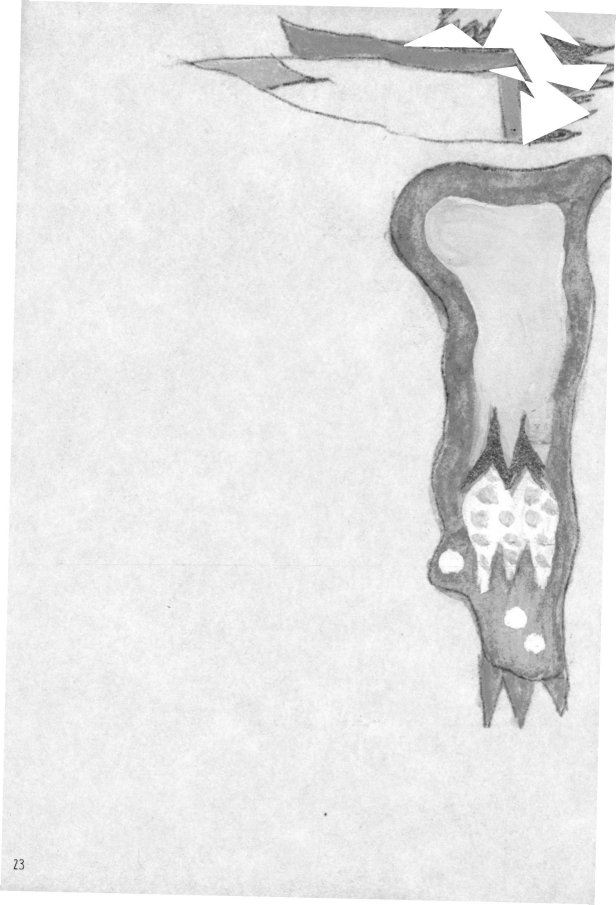

Being wrong

The one who admits to being wrong
finds the criminal
who regrets deeply not asking
the burning question
about the why of merciless loss

Farewell you inner companion

Farewell you inner companion
you preferred the mistress of alcohol
defiled my trust
and left me with this
eulogy for a dying friendship

How do you know

How do you know
that I wasn't dying inside
when I replied "Fine"
to your "How are you?"

Gold dust

Gold dust
on my hand
once tiny moth wings –
swatted

Gold dust
on my hand
Once tiny moth wings-

swatted

At the gate

Aware of being a statistic
it should not surprise me to be met by a reporter
at the gate:
"So what do you regret the most?"
the things I did not do
like the time I walked passed the house of the heart
I revered the most
he was standing out front gardening
perhaps with an expectant look of surprise on his face
I was seized by the feeling I was not the one he remembered
I dropped my glance and went on
now possessed with regret
that has lingered these seventy years
I think he might have been hurt

These advancing years

One's advancing years
should yield wiser answerings
mine only cutting questionings
tell me, who are you
who questions my every thought
ah... none other than my wiser self

Crash my heart

Crash my heart
against the sea wall
lest I drown
beneath the waves

Crush my heart
against the sea wall
lest I drown
beneath the
waves

I have heard it said

I have heard it said
grief subsides after seven years
the body may renew its skin
but how can the heart shed its shell

Family reunion

They all came
some I had not faced before
the twins
the extroverted playboy
the introverted nun
that meek self-effacing one with a will of steel
the romantic one-man woman
do not make a scene Lydia
the one who hid under the front porch
and cried silently when her feelings were hurt
who hated the mean teachers
and endured because of the few
who loved her thwarted selves

waiting
the appointed hour
your plane landed with a muffeled roar
but you were not
among the disembarking passengers
I waited, bewildered
suddenly a silver streak
pierced the darkened sky
way into the beyond
then I knew
you had taken the Heavenly Express

I was waiting
at the appointed hour
your plane landed with a most ...
but you were not among the disembarking
passengers
I waited, bewildered
Sudenly a silver streak
pierced the darkening skys into the beyond
then I knew
You had taken the Heavenly Express

The petal cool brow

On the petal cool brow
of new death
rest now the kiss
so long denied in life

I can keep the tears back

I can keep the tears back
until I hear the music
then the chords are loosened
and I can dance with you again

No exit

Dear moth
the beckoning moon deceives
cease batting your frail wings
against my sky light
there is no exit

Dear moth
the beckening moon deceives
cease battling your frail wings
against my sky light

there is no exit

If I find my mask

If I find my mask
I'll go dancing with the gypsies
all the indigo night

Ducks

Ducks with sapphire top knots
paddling away
elegant swans
loitering nonchalantly
both confronting the day
with enviable aplomb

I wonder as I wander

I wonder as I wander
on the platinum sands
of the havoc I created
the quivering beneath my feet
belies the terror of sand crabs
digging desperately to their uncertain fate

Russet leaves

Russet leaves
crisped by autumn
curling earthward
coverlets for slumbering seeds

Frog in my garden

The frog in my garden
complaining incessantly
his pond is leaking

Abalone

Abalone shell fragments
bespangle the
once-somebody's home

Mummy

Her
self
like an Egyptian mummy
lies buried
beneath yesterday's
dreams

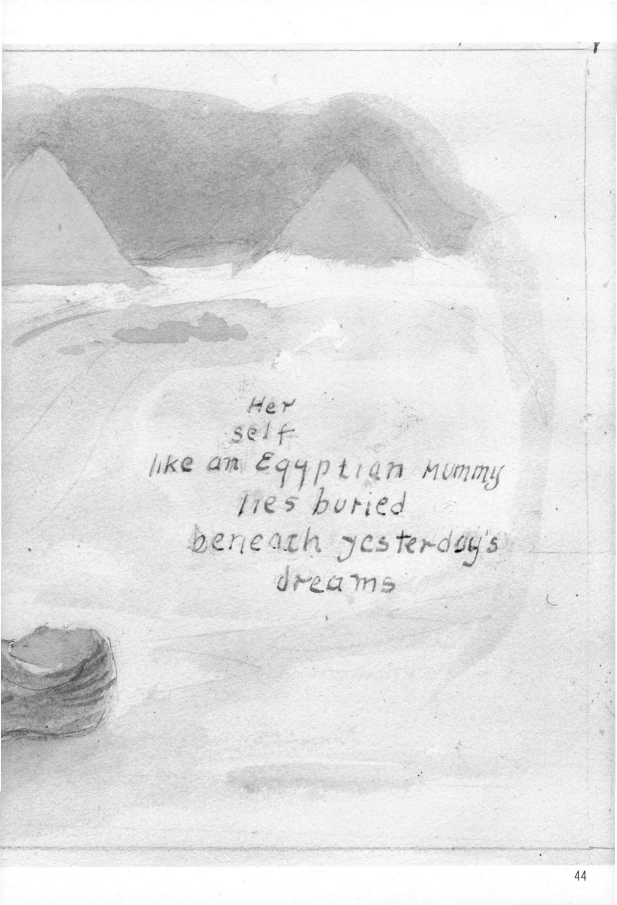

Her
self
like an Egyptian mummy
lies buried
beneath yesterday's
dreams

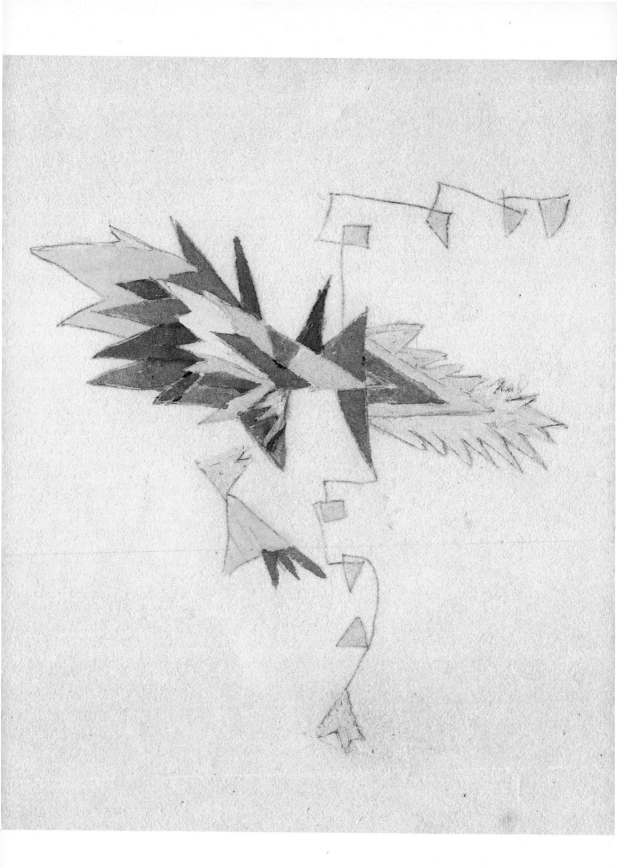

Butterfly

Tattered butterfly
who flung you in those thorny roses
wanton wind

Have you ever wished

Have you ever wished
you had taken the other path at the fork in the road
and imagined where you might be now
the darker passage
would he have been waiting for you
at this dark impasse

Why rush

Why rush
the tram is jammed
He won't be waiting
nor will he ever be
home sooner
it only makes the loneliness
that much longer
perhaps the noonday sun
will entice the winsome bud
in the window box to blossom
and a crimson rose will nod its welcome

One more dive

Beyond my depths
you say
but I haven't reached
bottom yet where
the nutrients
lie
Please, one more
dive

Beyond ? depths
you say?
but I haven't reached
bottom yet where
all the nutrients
lie
please, one more
dive

Afterword

"The privilege of a lifetime is being who you are"
—Joseph Campbell

Lydia Cooley Freeman off-handedly referred to these poems as "haikus." The venerable haiku has evolved over such a long period of time. Its signifying elements have been broken, revised, and reconstituted over and over again, and also torqued repeatedly through translations into multiple languages. Lydia was drawn to the pure haiku's simplicity and intimacy, its intense compactness, its visualness, directness, use of nature images as core, and especially the haiku's abrupt suddenness of closure. The most visual of poetic forms, the haiku appealed to Lydia as a painter.

With respect to function, I don't think she had much patience, tolerance, or discipline for the haiku. I say that as a compliment. The function of the haiku follows its form. There is usually no judging voice present. A good haiku is like a compelling documentary photograph. It speaks for itself, without any direct editorial comment or pose and steering by the poet. All the subjective content is left up to the reader. The haiku maker, selfless, remains a humble, restrained presence behind the scene. The function of the haiku traces to attendant moral traits prized in Japanese culture.

The haiku form was perfect for Lydia because it is so taut and visual, something we see in a few of the colorful geometric drawings that accompany the poems. There's an interesting cluster of three poems on page 41. They probably come as close to the pure form of the haiku as anywhere in the book. Or "Butterfly" on page 46. These are all strongly visual and rely on a central image. But they also enlighten, elaborate, question, and comment. The wind is "wanton." The frog is "complaining." Image and evaluation. As a poet, Lydia was interested in insight and engagement with her subjects. She had a lot she wanted to say about what she observed, felt, and remembered (and forgot, or even transgressed). In the Foreword Roy observes that Lydia's poems are a "record of one woman's confrontation and dance with her inner soul." Her "dances" are haiku in form only and otherwise poems in their confrontations, questionings, and regrets.

As I read these poems, I feel as if I am catching up with Lydia after a long absence in our friendship. I don't think I could have had this kind of conversation with her 35 years ago when my wife Christina and I lived next door to her in Santa Barbara and grew close in our daily contact. Now that I am in my 70s, I can meet her on common ground as she writes inside her numbered days.

I'm sure I would have had something to say back then on the "subjects" of her poems. Even a middle-aged man poised uneasily on the narrow beam of a precarious career could speak to Lydia's ruminations on old age, her confrontations with mortality and loss, and her tactful but honest grieving. I could have given her an earful on the seductions of alcohol consumption, the ills of American popular culture ("punctual on the unimportant," Lydia observes, "tardy on the essential"—such a surgical scalpel!), and the way she gets to know herself through her wholeness and complexity and inner conflicts, and her honest confrontations with her other selves—although I may have encouraged her to go a little easier on those darker parts that make "wretched company for / their guardian host." I think I knew back then a little about the rigors and the blindsidings of loving someone (no coupons, no returns, no shortcuts, no discounts), the superficialities we sometimes have to bear when loving someone, how "silent misunderstanding" betrays resentment and ruins friendship, etc. Although I know more now about the shadings between solitude, aloneness, and loneliness, I could have faked it when talking to her then about the poems "Why rush," "There was a time," "This solitude," and the many other places where she witnesses herself, late in life, standing apart, widowed, and still not belonging. I too had some "sorrows of the heart" to reveal. Who doesn't? For me such sharings were more forthcoming and less threatening when told to an older female confidant.

But what I could not have understood three decades ago is what Lydia's bravest poems—the ones with real integrity and honesty—are about. Old age brings no resolutions for the finitude, the unfinishedness, of our life experiences and journeys. The older you get, the persistent conundra only get more sharply defined while still defying resolution or solution. We are pretty well stuck in our fallibility. We end up in old age as finite and bounded as we are during any other period of our lives. (See "Angels," "I've heard it said,"

"These advancing years," "No exit," "Butterfly.") Not only is that okay, it is preferable to the default notion that life traces a single, noble trajectory up and then down. Life takes courage, humility, and grit all the time—certainly more so in old age. It is more spiral than arc. Our lives are complex swirls of celebrations and setbacks that repeat across the full span of our years. Tangles and knots untied and then bound up again. Perhaps this recognition of the perpetual unfinishedness and incompleteness of life was more of a shock to Lydia's generation than it is to mine. She was more inculcated by the notion of a grander narrative that there was a life cycle that looked like a bell curve. Middle age was the pinnacle, birth and old age were ascents and descents, etc. I don't think the alternative is unglamorous. We can have meaning, beauty, love and still live with moral ambiguity and the moving target of personal authenticity. Want completion, closure, and restitution? Go to the movies.

It took guts for Lydia to live her closing years in the same moral space — that realm of finitude and incompleteness, the place of "no exit" — that she occupied all her life. See the poem, page 37. Sure, the moon beckons—something tidal pulls us beyond our present moorings. But it is a deception, the moth batting its frail wings against her skylight (what a powerful image!). The moth is trapped between a past it cannot return to and a future that is uncertain (at best) and, at worst, an illusion distorted by the skylight. But that doesn't mean she cannot have meaning, love, and beauty—not at all.

A haiku by the 19th century Japanese poet Hanshin:
"There is neither heaven nor earth,
Only snow falling constantly."

Once Lydia befriended that mantle of finitude (she didn't always), she began to see everything else there is. Clearly, courageously, through the snow, just as it is.

—David Cooper, February 2022, Paso Robles, California